CLAPHAM Jn. to BECKENHAM Jn.
via CRYSTAL PALACE (LOW LEVEL)

Vic Mitchell and Keith Smith

MP Middleton Press

First published October 1994

ISBN 1 873793 36 7

© Middleton Press 1994

Design - Deborah Goodridge

Published by Middleton Press
                  Easebourne Lane
                  Midhurst
                  West Sussex
                  GU29 9AZ
                  Tel: (0730) 813169
(From 16 April 1995 - (01730) 813169)

Printed & bound by Biddles Ltd,
                  Guildford and Kings Lynn

CONTENTS

ACKNOWLEDGEMENTS

We are most grateful for the assistance received from so many of the photographers mentioned in the credits. We are also appreciative of the help given by R.M.Casserley, Dr.E.Course, G.Croughton, C.Hall J.R.W.Kirkby, K.Kiss, A.Ll.Lambert, N.Langridge, R.Randell, Mr.D. and Dr.S.Salter, N.Stanyon, M.Turvey and our ever supportive wives. Mrs M. Mason and Mr.D.Wallis have kindly allowed the use of photographs taken by the late E.Wallis.

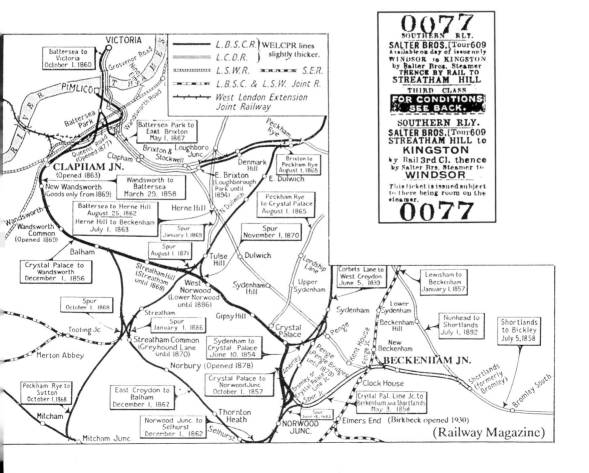

(Railway Magazine)

GEOGRAPHICAL SETTING

A gently sloping ridge runs from Wandsworth to Deptford, curving south and peaking near Crystal Palace. The route runs almost entirely on this clay formation, the summit being reached at the east end of Crystal Palace Tunnel.

All the maps in this volume are to the scale of 25" to 1 mile, unless otherwise noted.

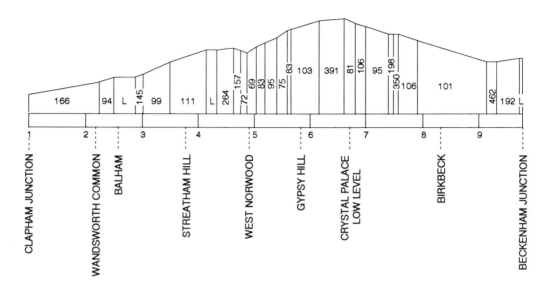

HISTORICAL BACKGROUND

The buildings of the 1851 Great Exhibition were reconstructed as the "Crystal Palace" on a rural South London hilltop in 1852-54. They formed the centre piece of a mass entertainment site that would today be termed a "theme park". For its success, a rail link to London was essential. This was provided by the London, Brighton and South Coast Railway which opened a branch from its London Bridge - East Croydon line at Sydenham on 10th June 1854. (The line conveyed freight from 27th March 1854). The project was very much inspired by the LBSCR as it and the Crystal Palace Company had a number of directors in common.

The LBSCR extended its operations from Crystal Palace to Wandsworth (Common) on 1st December 1856 by arrangement with the West End of London & Crystal Palace Junction Railway, which was incorporated by an Act of 4th August 1853. The word "junction" is normally omitted when referring to this company. (The ultimate goal of Victoria was reached in October 1860).

The third line to reach Crystal Palace was from the south at Norwood Junction, this route opening on 1st October 1857. It was built by the WELCPR and operated by the LBSCR.

The WELCPR opened a line from this route to Beckenham and Bromley (now Shortlands) on 3rd May 1858, operating a shuttle service from Crystal Palace using hired stock. The LBSCR purchased the WELCPR in 1859.

The London, Chatham and Dover Railway was the name of the East Kent Railway from 1st August 1859, this reflecting the small company's intention to reach London on a route not owned by its rival, the South Eastern Railway. Its trains began to run to Victoria on 3rd October 1860. The shuttle trains were discontinued but the LCDR did not carry passengers from stations west of Crystal Palace to that station or vice versa. Their more direct route via Herne Hill was completed in 1863 and most LCDR trains used that line thereafter.

A shuttle service between Beckenham Junction and Norwood Junction was introduced by the LCDR on 18th June 1862, this operating until 1917. From 1863 the LCDR and the LBSCR operated jointly a shuttle service between Beckenham Junction and Crystal Palace. This ceased on 1st December 1915. This part of the route was revived on 3rd March 1929 when it was electrified. The opening dates of the lines adjacent to the route of this book are shown on the map on the previous page.

The LCDR was operated by a managing committee from 1st January 1899 (along with the South Eastern Railway), the combination becoming known as the South Eastern & Chatham Railway. This, together with LBSCR and other lines, became part of the Southern Railway on 1st January 1923. The lines were nationalised as part of British Railways on 1st January 1948.

Electrification

The LBSCR introduced electric trains between Victoria and Crystal Palace via Balham on 12th May 1911, this service being extended to Norwood Junction and Selhurst on 1st June 1912. Overhead wires at 6700 volts AC were used throughout.

Trains using conductor rails at 660 volts DC were introduced as follows -

London Bridge to Crystal Palace
            via Sydenham   25 March 1928
Victoria to Beckenham Junction
            via Balham   3 March 1929

The latter replaced the overhead system from Victoria to Crystal Palace. The Crystal Palace - Norwood Junction line was also converted at the same time.

PASSENGER SERVICES

In January 1860 there were 23 weekday and 11 Sunday trains each way over the WELCPR and in October of that year they were increased to 27 and 12 and extended to London Bridge.

Services developed remarkably in terms of frequency, origination and termination. London termini included Victoria, London Bridge, Kensington (Addison Road) and eventually Holborn Viaduct. Details would demand much space and make tedious reading. We will therefore confine our comments mainly to the more unusual section east of Crystal Palace.

The LCDR/LBSCR joint operation offered a shuttle service of four weekday trains in 1869, this increasing to 12 by the time of its cessation in 1915. Upon electrification in 1929, three trains per hour were on offer (betwen Victoria and Beckenham Junction). This was curtailed and a shuttle arrangement was re-established during World War II and again from September 1958 until June 1960. A weekday frequency of half-hourly has usually been maintained although it was reduced to hourly during the middle of the day in the 1985-90 period.

Regular through trains between South and North London were discontinued during World War I, not to appear again until 16th May 1988 under the brand name of "Thameslink". A Purley - Luton service called at Crystal Palace, Gipsy Hill and West Norwood hourly from that date and a service from Guildford was introduced in May 1990. It operated for only four years.

June 1869

CLAPHAM JUNCTION

1. This now important junction station opened on 1st March 1863, nearly three years after the line to Victoria was completed. This is the view towards London soon after the turn of the century with the London & South Western Railway's original two lines (left), the LBSCR's three in the centre (note the shorter single faced platform for the centre one) and the West London Extension Railway's two. These are seen on the extreme right and are now numbered 16 and 17. (National Railway Museum)

2. A further view of the station at about the same time includes a down LBSCR train with a class D1 0-4-2T. All the structures seen here were demolished in 1903-05 in connection with the quadrupling of both main lines. Coaches are standing on the LSWR's third through line beyond the porte-cochère covering the approach road. Its Windsor lines were further north. (National Railway Museum)

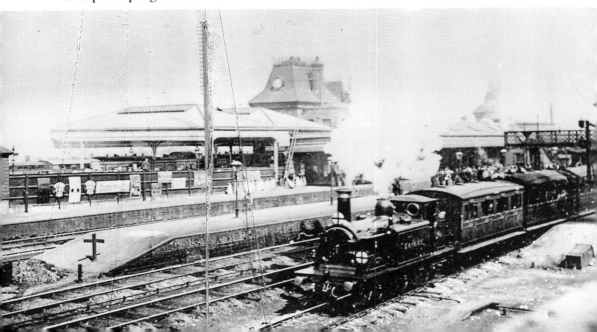

3. The open lattice footbridge recorded in the previous pictures was replaced by the wide, covered and glazed structure still in use today. This excursion to Hastings was photographed on 9th April 1928, the locomotive being "Gladstone" class B1 no. B179 of 1890 construction. The engine and the overhead wires would all cease to be used in 1929. (H.C.Casserley)

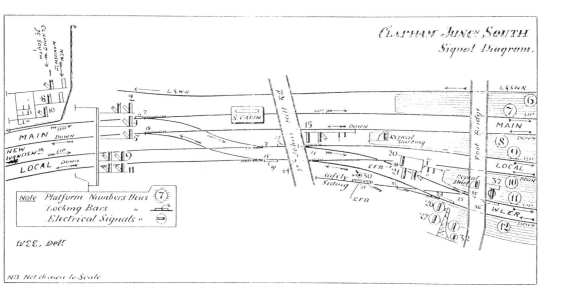

4. The WLER came into use on the same day that the station opened. These are the starting signals on its down platform in 1928, the arms consisting of appropriately coloured fabric on wire frames with back lighting. They remained in use until 1952. The shunt signal is off for the engine run-round siding. Many milk churns changed trains here. (Late E.Wallis)

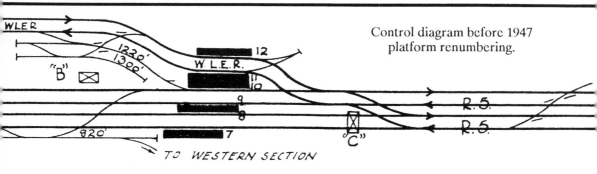

Control diagram before 1947
platform renumbering.

5. The photographer is standing on the former boundary between LBSCR and LSWR property in January 1931, the platforms then being numbered 6 and 7. At no. 6 is class M7 0-4-4T no. E58 and between 7 & 8 are the redundant and wireless electrification gantries. (H.C.Casserley)

6. A down freight rumbles along the former LBSCR main line, while another waits near the site of the signal seen in picture no. 4. Colour light signals were introduced in this area on 12th October 1952, when the LBSCR South Box ("C" Box in SR and BR days) was closed. It was situated across the road behind the camera. (Lens of Sutton)

7. The 11.40am Victoria to West Croydon via Streatham Hill is leaving platform 15 (formerly 10) on 31st October 1954. The platforms were renumbered on 16th November 1947. The sharply curved local platforms are right of centre in the previous picture. (D.Cullum)

8. The partial rebuilding of St. John's Hill bridge was recorded from platform 12 on 6th September 1966. On the right of this picture (and the left of no. 6) is the covered footbridge that replaced the roadway seen in picture no. 1. The bridge was closed at the beginning of World War II and used as a commercial training school for railway staff. On the right of this picture and no. 6 are former booking offices. (D.Cullum)

9. An inter-regional freight comes off the West London Line on 29th June 1977, hauled by no. 25069. Conductor rails were laid through platforms 16 and 17 (formerly 11 and 12) in 1968 and on to the WLL in 1993. A vestige of the former short siding remains in front of the locomotive. (J.Scrace)

10. The sole remaining locomotive hauled daily service in south-east England in 1994 was between Brighton and Manchester (Edinburgh on Sundays). The 09.20 from Brighton creeps in on 1st January 1994 to pick up the miniature tram driver who was destined for Olympia, where he would drive the quarter scale Middleton Press tramcar round the gallery. The locomotive is no. 47825 *Thomas Telford* - the great road transport advocate. (V.Mitchell)

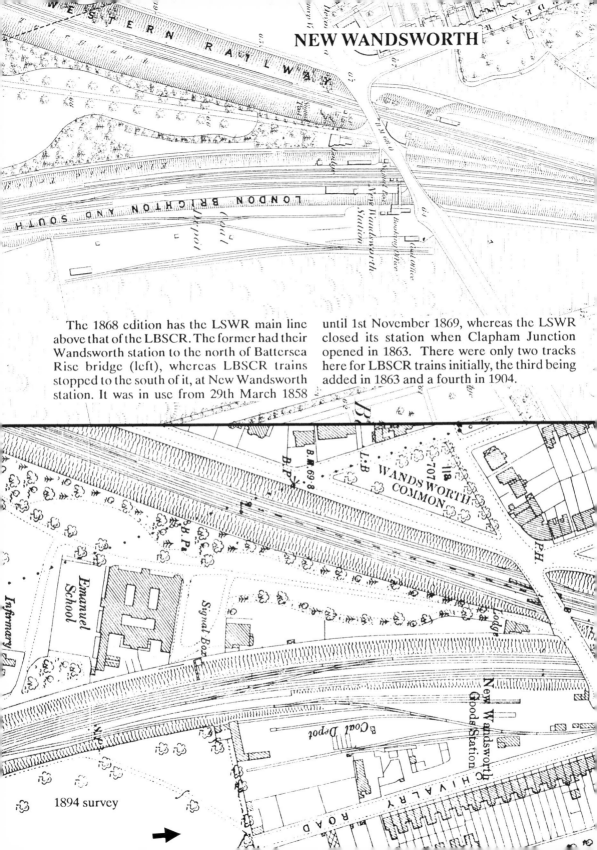

NEW WANDSWORTH

The 1868 edition has the LSWR main line above that of the LBSCR. The former had their Wandsworth station to the north of Battersea Rise bridge (left), whereas LBSCR trains stopped to the south of it, at New Wandsworth station. It was in use from 29th March 1858 until 1st November 1869, whereas the LSWR closed its station when Clapham Junction opened in 1863. There were only two tracks here for LBSCR trains initially, the third being added in 1863 and a fourth in 1904.

1894 survey

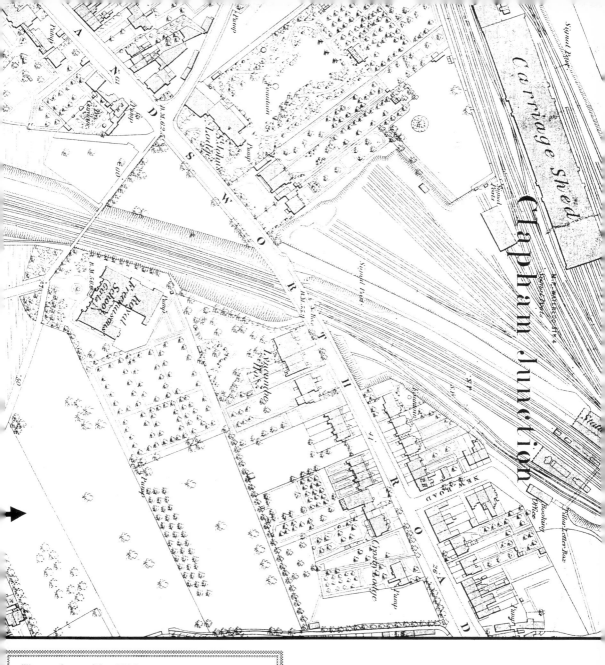

The good news May 1994 -

A Clapham Junction - Olympia - Willesden Junction service is introduced. It comprises a 30 minute interval timetable Monday to Fridays only, operated by two-car "Heritage" DMUs from platform 2.

The bad news May 1994 -

Manchester trains are no longer shown on departure boards as the former are operated by InterCity and the latter are compiled by South West Trains. This great disservice to passengers is widely practised now and is consequent to the Government's ill conceived scheme for railway fragmentation.

Maps and photographs of other parts of Clapham Junction can be found in the companion albums *Victoria to East Croydon*, *Waterloo to Windsor* **and** *Waterloo to Woking.*

11. Battersea Rise bridge is in the background as class D1 0-4-2T no. B216 approaches New Wandsworth signal box on 17th March 1928.

The coal depot is on the elevated ground on the right. The yard closed on 7th October 1968. (H.C.Casserley)

12. New Wandsworth signal box is behind the signals and is also marked on the map. The signals are repeaters to the elevated ones mounted high on the adjacent white posts.

They are marked on the left of the Clapham Junction South Box diagram. Part of the coal depot is on the right of this 1933 photograph. (Late E.Wallis)

13. No. 73142 has just passed under Battersea Rise on 1st July 1986, while hauling royal train coaches from Gatwick Airport on the occasion of an official visit by the President of West Germany. (J.Scrace)

14. The Crawley to Merehead Quarry empties passes the site of the coal depot on 19th March 1992. Yeoman-owned no. 59004 will travel via the WLL to reach the former GWR main line near Acton. (J.Scrace)

WANDSWORTH COMMON

15. The first station was a modest timber construction and was in use as a terminus from 1st December 1856 until 29th March 1858. High class housing development in the area justified the provision of a new station on 1st November 1869. It had three platforms from the outset, a fourth being added in 1904. Rebuilding was completed in 1907, this being the view from the south when three tracks were in use.
(Lens of Sutton)

16. Wandsworth Common presented an ideal location for train photography. This down Portsmouth express was hauled by class D1 no. 33 *Mitcham* of 1876 and class B2 4-4-0 no. 315 *Duncannon* of 1895. Here they are climbing at 1 in 94. (Lens of Sutton)

17. At almost the same location, K class 2-6-0 no. 337 adds to London's grime on 11th November 1927. Unlike modern overhead electrification, the copper conductor was sus- pended from *two* steel wires. Coal wagons occupy the headshunt, the new retaining wall for which was seen in the previous picture. (H.C.Casserley)

18.   A southward view under Nightingale Lane bridge on 5th July 1930 includes the down main starting signal repeating banner (black), a temporary speed sign (green) and an up local train from Coulsdon North to Victoria. (Late E.Wallis)

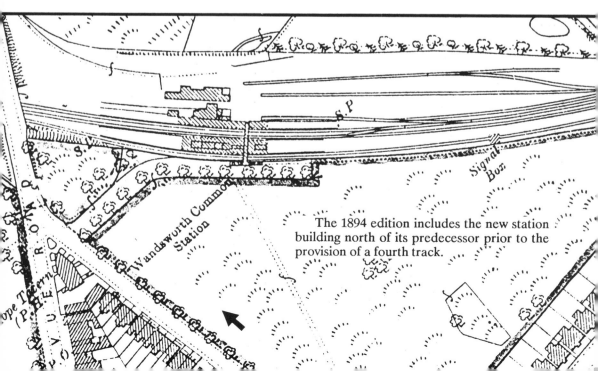

The 1894 edition includes the new station building north of its predecessor prior to the provision of a fourth track.

19. Included in this picture (centre) is the signal seen in the previous view. North Box (which was built during World War I but never opened) is on the right and on the left are the photographer's wife and daughter. Being a signal engineer he had authority to climb the tall signals then common. (Late E.Wallis)

20. Signalling transition was recorded on 21st September 1952, as was one high-sided coke wagon amongst all the coal wagons. Note the hut and fireplace for fog signalmen whose services would no longer be required with the change from oil lamps to bright coloured lights. (D.Cullum)

21. The crossover on the local lines (centre) was seldom used and the once busy coal yard closed on 28th September 1964. The use of coal for domestic purposes ceased in the London area owing to legislation following the disastrous smogs of the early 1950s. (Lens of Sutton)

22. The smart chocolate and cream liveried "Brighton Belle" was repainted in blue and grey in 1969 and fitted wih BR logos as seen. The train generally used the main line but was diverted onto the down local on 8th May 1969. The full set of platform canopies was then still in place. (J.Scrace)

23. The up main and down local canopies had been lost by the time that 4SUB no. 4732 arrived on 7th September 1982. It is working the 12.14 Victoria to Beckenham Junction. The last regular use of a 4SUB was on 1st October 1983. (J.Scrace)

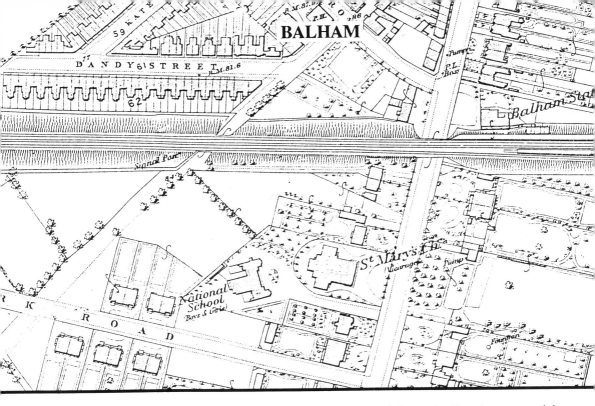

BALHAM

24. The station opened with the WELCPR on 1st December 1856, the main buildings being on the north side of the line in a turning off Balham High Road. Electric trams arriving on this highway in May 1903 took away many former railway passengers. (Lens of Sutton)

The first edition of 1868 reveals the rural nature of Balham at that time and that the third track to London ran from the Croydon branch (lower right). Note the space on Bedford Hill bridge (right) ready for the fourth track.

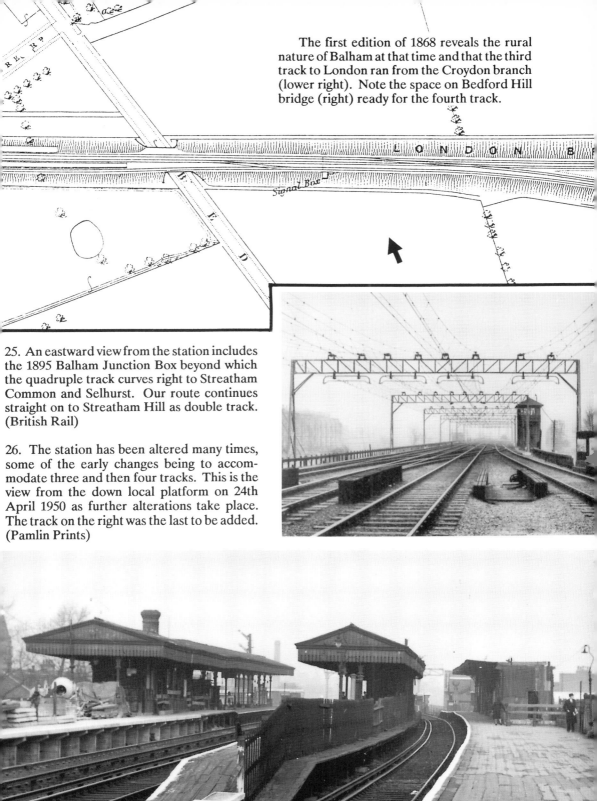

25. An eastward view from the station includes the 1895 Balham Junction Box beyond which the quadruple track curves right to Streatham Common and Selhurst. Our route continues straight on to Streatham Hill as double track. (British Rail)

26. The station has been altered many times, some of the early changes being to accommodate three and then four tracks. This is the view from the down local platform on 24th April 1950 as further alterations take place. The track on the right was the last to be added. (Pamlin Prints)

27. Chaos reigns .... by 11th November 1951 work was in progress on the up local platform. S4528 is forming a Beckenham Junction to Victoria service. Note that the platforms were still gas lit. (Pamlin Prints)

28. By 6th March 1954 work was in hand to eliminate the awkward platform arrangement and provide two island platforms. The fence reduced the risk of passengers alighting from the wrong side of down local trains. (D.Cullum)

29. Following completion of the work, a modern design of steel framed canopy was erected. Few trains stopped at the main line platforms. A timber platform was retained to minimise weight on the embankment. (Pamlin Prints)

30. The new canopy on the local platforms and a Ford Popular were recorded in the 1960s. The buildings show little change from when picture no. 24 was taken. (British Rail)

31. An eastward view from Balham Junction Box includes its shadow and its successor. The latter was in use from 12th October 1952 until 7th June 1981, when Victoria Panel assumed control of the area. To the left of the new box is Streatham Hill carriage washing plant. The 1862 direct route to East Croydon is on the right. (Pamlin Prints)

STREATHAM HILL

32. The station opened with the line on 1st December 1856 as simply "Streatham". The suffix was added on 1st September 1868 as "Streatham" was soon applied to a new station on the Peckham Rye - Sutton line. (Lens of Sutton)

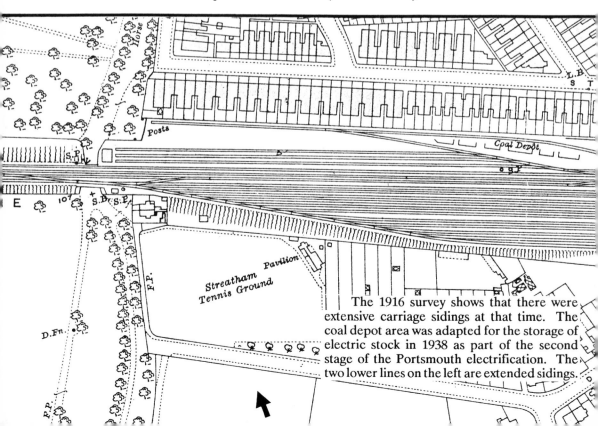

The 1916 survey shows that there were extensive carriage sidings at that time. The coal depot area was adapted for the storage of electric stock in 1938 as part of the second stage of the Portsmouth electrification. The two lower lines on the left are extended sidings.

33. The station was well situated on the main road where serious competition arrived on 19th June 1904 in the form of an electric tramway operated by London County Council. The station suffered a near miss from a Zeppelin's bomb in World War I. (Lens of Sutton)

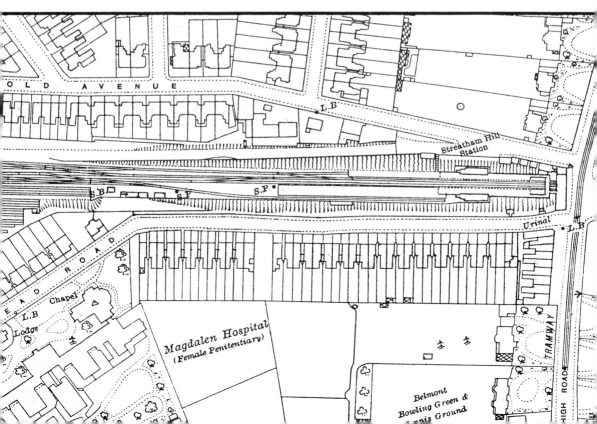

34.   A 1953 photograph includes the up bay platform which was authorised for passenger use although it had no white edging. Trains starting from this station in 1954 were at 6.18, 6.38, 6.58, 7.18, 7.38 and 7.58 am, weekdays only. (Pamlin Prints)

35. Centre in this 1956 westward view is the 1898 signal box which closed on 19th November 1967. Mechanical and electrical signalling is in use. No trains commenced their journeys here at that time. (D.Cullum)

36. In the distance in this 1957 eastward view is the 443yd long Leigham Court tunnel, which is on a 1 in 111 up gradient. Lack of paint was a widespread problem at that time.
(British Rail)

37. On 9th June 1978, no. 33035 heads a north bound parcels train, while unit no. 5041 works the 11.13 Victoria to Beckenham Junction. Note the number of crossovers still required. (J.Scrace)

38. The 09.30 Temple Mills to Norwood Junction freight included some railway bogies on 9th June 1978. No. 37049 is in charge. Electric stock is berthed in the background in the 1938 sidings. (J.Scrace)

39. When photographed in 1993, the simple street-level building had changed little in the previous 90 years or more. Back in 1903 the station received four LNWR trains each way on weekdays, working between Croydon (New) and Willesden Junction via Chelsea. (J.Scrace)

40. This and the next three photographs were taken in August 1993 to illustrate rolling stock variety. Class 456 reliability was improving and no. 456023 was recorded working the 12.00 West Croydon to Victoria service on the 15th. (M.J.Stretton)

41. The first of the class 456 units was delivered in December 1990, one of 24 two-car sets; each set is provided with a toilet. Built by BREL Ltd., each pair of coaches seats 151 passengers. Note the differing lengths of the two sheds. (M.J.Stretton)

42. Class 319 units (left and centre in the sidings) were introduced in 1987 for the Thameslink services and include pantographs for use on the overhead wires north of the Thames. Class 455 units are also evident among the weeds. (M.J.Stretton)

43. Nearest the camera in the shorter shed is a 1978 universal tamper and liner from Three Bridges. Beyond it is a GP-Tramm (General purpose track and rail maintenance machine) which was based at Streatham Hill. Only inspection and minor repairs of berthed stock was undertaken here. (M.J.Stretton)

EAST OF STREATHAM HILL

44. Leigham Junction down signals were for the Tulse Hill line (left) and the Crystal Palace route (right). When the striped arm was off, a "W" (for warning) appeared on a slide in the black box indicating that the section was clear but that the junction was blocked. (J.Scrace)

45. This and the previous picture were taken a few days before the box closed on 13th April 1969. It had opened in 1871. East of the junction our route passes over the Tulse Hill - Mitcham Junction line. (J.Scrace)

←

46. A down train runs towards Crystal Palace on the 19-chain curve between Leigham Junction and West Norwood Junction, a section that justified check rails. (D.Cullum coll.)

47. The check rails ended at West Norwood Junction, seen here in this 1949 westward view. The route we are taking from Streatham Hill is on the left and that from Tulse Hill is on the right. (D.Cullum)

48. York Hill bridge was dangerously narrow for motor traffic and was spectacularly demolished in the early hours of 14th June 1958. The parapets and roadbed had been removed from the bridge previously. Ironically, German V1 flying bombs exploded either side of the bridge in 1944 (on 27th July and 22nd August) but without demolishing it. (British Rail)

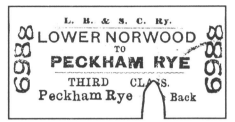

49. Local residents had been notified of the impending explosion and some came out to view the result from the parallel footbridge. See how accurately the sleeper decking had been placed. (British Rail)

50. Next day, much shovelling completed the operation. Note that loose coupled wagons without continuous brakes were then used for such work. Picture 48 was taken from the shelter by the signal. (R.C.Riley)

51. A 1956 westward view from Canterbury Grove bridge reveals that the junction was almost under Lansdowne Hill bridge, which was of an unusual design as it carried a road junction. (D.Cullum)

52. One window of this box is visible in the previous picture. It ceased to function on 13th April 1969. The architecture suggests that this was a wartime replacement. (J.Scrace)

53. Carrying the sign WILLESDEN, an LNWR "Watford" tank heads a train from Croydon (New) and was photographed from Lansdowne Hill bridge. The footbridge in the background links Canterbury Grove. St. Luke's Church is on the left. (R.S.Carpenter coll.)

54. These are West Norwood Junction up signals in 1952. They are situated at the end of a 21-chain curve, south of Canterbury Grove footbridge. The 4SUB is working a circular tour from London Bridge, via Sydenham, Crystal Palace and Tulse Hill. (Pamlin Prints)

0000
SOUTHERN RAILWAY.
CHEAP DAY
Available as advertised.
London Bridge
Via Crystal Palace (L.L.) &
or Waterloo
Via Clapham Junction TO
GIPSY HILL
Third Class
FOR CONDITIONS
SEE BACK.
SOUTHERN RAILWAY.
CHEAP DAY
Available as advertised.
Gipsy Hill to
LONDON BRIDGE
Via Crystal Palace (L.L.)
or WATERLOO
Via Clapham Junction
Third Class
0000

8992

L. B. & C. RY.
Available on the DATE of issue ONLY.
This Ticket is issued subject to the Regulations
& Conditions stated in the Company's Time
Tables & Bills.
GIPSY HILL
TO
Tulse Hill. th
1½d. THIRD CLASS. 1½d.

8992

0163

L. B. & S. C. & L. & N. W. RYS.
Available on the DATE of issue ONLY
STREATHAM HILL TO   BERKHAMSTED
Via Clapham Junc. & Kensington or Via Victoria
& Kensington by L. & N. W. or District Rys.
or Via London & Euston.
2s. 6½d. THIRD CLASS. 2s. 6½d.
The connection of trains not guaranteed.
Not Transferable.   Issued subject to the
Conditions in the Time Tables of the respective
Co's over whose lines this ticket is available.
BERKHAMSTED
SING

0163

WEST NORWOOD

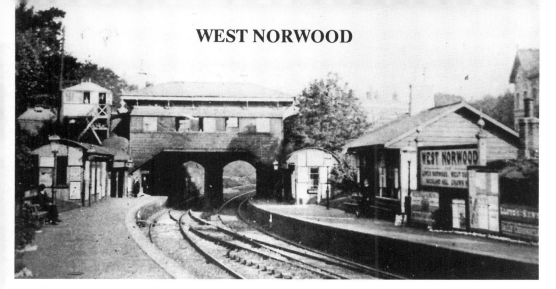

55. The station opened with the line as "Lower Norwood" and was renamed on 1st January 1886. Agitation from new residents who objected to being "lower" resulted in the meaningless "West" being applied. The curved-roof buildings probably date from the opening. The timber-clad offices spanning the tracks are thought to have followed. Their successors are behind them and date from 1891. These would have obstructed the view from the lofty signal box. (Lens of Sutton)

56. The revised position for the signal box is apparent in this unusual picture of AC cable installation. The box opened in 1892 and closed on 25th March 1928. (Lens of Sutton)

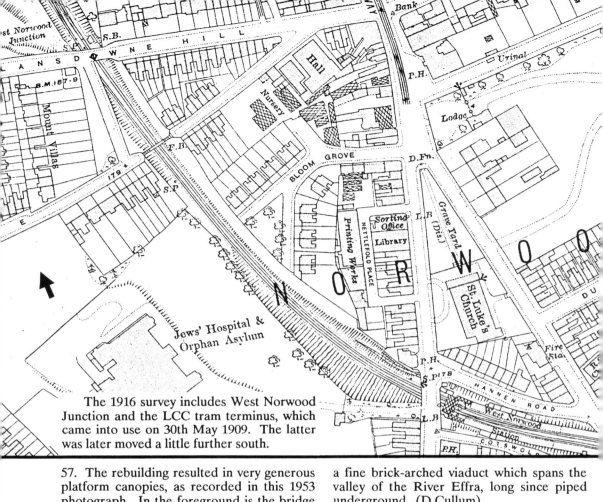

The 1916 survey includes West Norwood Junction and the LCC tram terminus, which came into use on 30th May 1909. The latter was later moved a little further south.

57. The rebuilding resulted in very generous platform canopies, as recorded in this 1953 photograph. In the foreground is the bridge over Norwood High Street. Here commences a fine brick-arched viaduct which spans the valley of the River Effra, long since piped underground. (D.Cullum)

58. The bridge carrying Knights Hill over the railway was widened by only a few feet. On the left an inspector stands between the brick and steel sections. The line dips down at 1 in 72 and up at 1 in 69 under this bridge. (British Rail)

←

59. The Acton-Norwood Junction freights have had a variety of diesel locomotives over the years, ranging from "Westerns" to class 47s, 50s and to no. 31422 on 19th August 1982. (J.S.Petley)

←

60. All the Victorian structures vanished in 1969 in favour of this small street level CLASP building together with the shelters and footbridge seen in the adjacent pictures. (J.Scrace)

61. The reversal from 17 to 43 chain curvature is evident as no. 456004 is viewed from the footbridge on 22nd July 1993. It is working the 14.03 West Croydon to London Bridge via Tulse Hill. (J.Scrace)

GIPSY HILL

62. This fine eastward view includes the roof-line and one of the towers of the Crystal Palace, together with two of the many LBSCR round-ended wagons used with tarpaulins. As with most other intermediate stations, this one opened with the line. (Lens of Sutton)

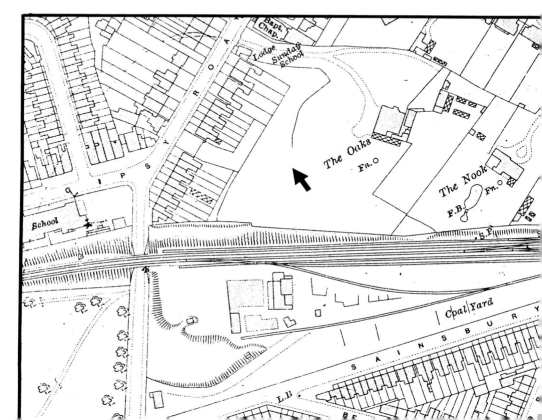

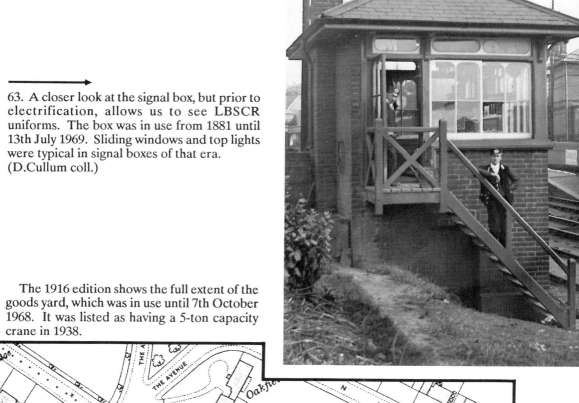

63. A closer look at the signal box, but prior to electrification, allows us to see LBSCR uniforms. The box was in use from 1881 until 13th July 1969. Sliding windows and top lights were typical in signal boxes of that era. (D.Cullum coll.)

The 1916 edition shows the full extent of the goods yard, which was in use until 7th October 1968. It was listed as having a 5-ton capacity crane in 1938.

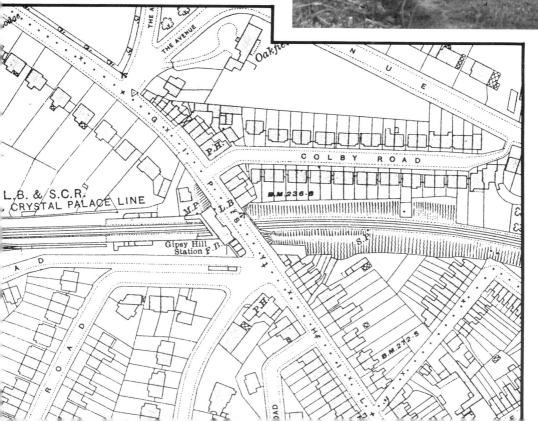

64. Shortly after the provision of conductor rails in 1928, class I3 4-4-2T no. B89 was recorded working a London Bridge - Crystal Palace train. This had run via Tulse Hill and was normally electrically operated. (Lens of Sutton)

65. Gipsy Hill is the name of the road that crosses the railway here. The picture dates from about 1930. The whole area of West and Upper Norwood was once just a vast piece of common land on the edge of the Great North Wood and and for well over two hundred years home to a large number of Romany folk or Gipsies who are remembered by various road names in the area. The famous Queen of the Gipsies, Margaret Finch (1636-1740), lived in a house where "The Oaks" is shown on the map. (British Rail)

66. Few platform running-in boards listed so many districts. East of the station is the 746yd-long Crystal Palace Tunnel, sometimes known as Gipsy Hill Tunnel. Subsidence therein in 1938 resulted in single line working and termination here of most trains from London Bridge via Tulse Hill. This necessitated provision of a starting signal at the west end of the down platform for most of that year. The deformation of the tunnel was caused by the great volume of water used during the Crystal Palace fire in 1936. (H.C.Casserley coll.)

68. Inter-regional freight transfer traffic was still heavy when no. D5184 was pictured climbing the 1 in 103 gradient on 10th October 1964. It was working a Willesden Junction to Norwood Junction service. The building once housed AC equipment probably a section box. (J.N.Faulkner)

67. The "Essex Wealdman" was an unusual ramblers excursion from Clapham Junction to Ongar on 28th September 1958. It picked up passengers at Streatham Hill, West Norwood, Crystal Palace, Forest Hill and New Cross Gate and reversed at Liverpool Street. Class M7 0-4-4T no. 30322 was used for the first part of the journey. (J.H.Aston)

69. A photograph from March 1969 reveals that the goods sidings had just been lifted but that the down refuge siding was still in place. The box would close within a few months. (J.Scrace)

70. Steel from Sheerness Steelworks passes through on 7th March 1992 destined for South Wales - a modern case of "Coals to Newcastle". This train normally ran via Herne Hill but was diverted due to engineering works. (C.Wilson)

71. NSE seating and timepieces are evident as a class 455 forms the 12.50 Victoria to Beckenham Junction on 7th March 1992. This unit had been fitted with dot matrix indicators but reversion to blinds did not stop misleading information being given. (C.Wilson)

72. Much smarter than in picture 65, the exterior has lost its symmetry with the insertion of a shop window, but at least the crests had been neatly picked out in appropriate colours in 1993. (J.Scrace)

73. Provision of trains with good acceleration and toilets was compensation for loss of platform comforts. The down side canopy and building had been demolished in December 1980. No. 456009 is bound for West Croydon on 1st July 1993. (J.Scrace)

The 1872 map at 6" to 1 mile has Crystal Palace (Low Level) station top left with the 1854 line to Sydenham curving to the right. Diagonally across the page is the route from London Bridge to East Croydon (illustrated in a Middleton Press album of that title). South from Crystal Palace is the 1857 route to Norwood Junction. Curving across the lower part of the page is the LCDR line to Beckenham Junction that we will follow. The spur linking the two dates from 1862. In the top right corner is the LCDR's Penge station, later known as Penge East.

CRYSTAL PALACE

74. The terminus was situated in this vicinity in 1854-56 and a two-span roof was erected between the two massive walls. Part of the Crystal Palace and one of its towers are in the background. (Lens of Sutton)

The motive for staging the Great Exhibition in 1851 was to provide a show much larger and more prestigious than the periodic Paris Exhibitions. It was not only to display British products of the Industrial Revolution but art in all its forms, and every nation was invited to participate, including the French.

A temporary building of massive proportions was to be erected in Hyde Park and a novel design by Joseph Paxton was accepted by the organisers. It was based on the lily house that he had built close to Chatsworth House in Derbyshire. Clad entirely in glass, the 18 acre building was soon jocularly described as the "Crystal Palace" by *Punch*. Over 2000 men had erected it in under nine months, the pillars and cross-ribs being of iron and the sash bars of timber. The 100,000 exhibits were contained in eleven miles of stalls on two floors - astounding statistics.

After the exhibition closed on 14th October 1851, the Crystal Palace Company was formed, its directors including Samual Laing (LBSCR chairman), Sir Joseph Paxton and Leo Schuster (LBSCR director and owner of a 280 acre estate at Sydenham Hill). The latter parted with his land so that the Crystal Palace could be rebuilt in sylvan surroundings and the LBSCR could convey thousands of passengers to visit the permanent exhibition and the countless special events proposed.

The building was reconstructed on an even more lavish scale, with six floors instead of two. Queen Victoria performed the opening ceremony on 10th June 1854. For thirty years, over two million people visited the site annually, almost all by rail. The attractions were extended to include a sea water aquarium and a flying machine by Hiram Maxim, while transitory events included pet shows of every type, ballooning, firework displays, trade shows and massed meetings of every imaginable organisation. In addition, circuses, concerts, wrestling, athletic events, music festivals and pantomimes kept the railways busy throughout the year.

The 1911 "Festival of Empire" was so extensive that a narrow gauge electric railway linked the various national displays but that year saw the company bankrupt. In 1913, trustees took over but WWI brought closure and Naval occupation. Years of neglect of the buildings, gardens and famous statues were never to be fully overcome but the public was readmitted in 1920. Many notable events were held but the Palace had lost much of its appeal and public tastes had changed, railway revenue declining in consequence. Disaster struck on 30th November 1936, when the entire structure (except the two towers) was destroyed by fire. Subsequently, outdoor events have generated some peaks in rail travel, but traffic figures have been slight in comparison with the heydays.

75. A new station house (centre) and offices (left) were built over the tracks in 1875. In the left background is part of the covered way to the Palace itself. (Lens of Sutton)

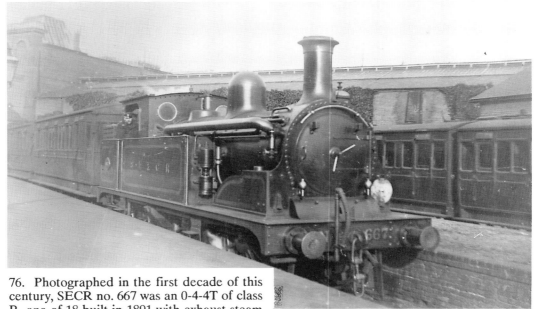

76. Photographed in the first decade of this century, SECR no. 667 was an 0-4-4T of class R, one of 18 built in 1891 with exhaust steam pipes leading into the side tanks. It is standing at platform 6 waiting to work a train to Beckenham Junction, a service which the LBSCR worked jointly with the SECR.
(Lens of Sutton)

77. The platforms were numbered 1 to 8 from north to south. Standing at platform 5 in September 1913 is a push-pull train waiting to make its three mile journey to Beckenham Junction. (D.Cullum coll.)

The 1894 6" scale map shows the full extent of the park and includes the LBSCR Penge station (lower right and later "Penge West") and also Sydenham station (extreme right). The LCDR's 1865 High Level station is on the left, this being fully described and extensively illustrated in our companion album, *Crystal Palace and Catford Loop*.

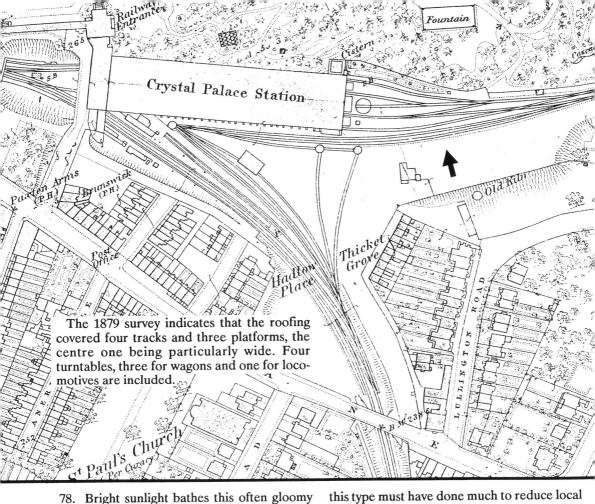

The 1879 survey indicates that the roofing covered four tracks and three platforms, the centre one being particularly wide. Four turntables, three for wagons and one for locomotives are included.

78. Bright sunlight bathes this often gloomy location at the east end of Crystal Palace Tunnel. The introduction of electric trains of this type must have done much to reduce local pollution. (D.Cullum coll.)

DOWN SPECIAL TRAINS TO CRYSTAL PALACE L.B. & S.C.R.

Company's train.	From.	Booked arrival time.	Actual time of arrival.
L. & S.W.R.	Putney	10.30 a.m.	10.32 a.m.
L. & N.W.R.	Queen's Park	10.33 ,,	10.36 ,,
N.L.R.	Hackney	10.50 ,,	10.47 ,,
L.B. & S.C.R.	Victoria	10.56 ,,	10.59 ,,
N.L.R.	Homerton	11.2 ,,	10.54 ,,
L.B. & S.C.R.	Victoria	11.14 ,,	11.19 ,,
N.L.R.	Dalston	11.14 ,,	11.3 ,,
,,	Canonbury	11.21 ,,	11.11 ,,
L.B. & S.C.R.	Victoria	11.37 ,,	11.41 ,,
N.L.R.	Hackney	11.38 ,,	11.34 ,,
L.B. & S.C.R.	Clapham Junction	11.44 ,,	11.41 ,,
N.L.R.	Homerton	11.50 ,,	11.38 ,,
L.B. & S.C.R.	Clapham Junction	11.56 ,,	11.52 ,,
,, ,,	Peckham Rye	11.57 ,,	11.55 ,,
N.L.R.	Dalston	12.2 p.m.	11.49 ,,
L.B. & S.C.R.	Peckham Rye	12.7 ,,	12.7 p.m.
G.W.R.	Westbourne Park	12.8 ,,	11.58 a.m.
L.B. & S.C.R.	Wandsworth Common	12.14 ,,	12.19 p.m.
G.W.R.	Paddington	12.20 ,,	12.16 ,,
L.B. & S.C.R.	Peckham Rye and North Dulwich	12.26 ,,	12.25 ,,
G.W.R.	Paddington	12.32 ,,	12.29 ,,
L.B. & S.C.R	Clapham Junction	12.38 ,,	12.35 ,,
G.W.R.	Paddington	12.44 ,,	12.39 ,,
L.B. & S.C.R.	Tooting	12.48 ,,	12.48 ,,
,, ,,	Kensington (Addison Road)	1.2 ,,	12.51 ,,
,, ,,	,, ,,	1.17 ,,	1.11 ,,
,, ,,	,, ,,	1.22 ,,	1.21 ,,
,, ,,	,, ,,	1.32 ,,	1.30 ,,
,, ,,	West Brompton	1.43 ,,	1.38 ,,

No. of train.	Company's train.	From.	Booked arrival time.	Actual time of arrival.
30	L.B. & S.C.R.	Chelsea	1.58 p.m.	1.55 p.m.
31	,, ,,	West Brompton	2.3 ,,	1.59 ,,
32	,, ,,	Chelsea	2.13 ,,	2.9 ,,
33	,, ,,	Streatham Hill	2.20 ,,	2.16 ,,
34	,, ,,	Balham	2.28 ,,	2.26 ,,
47	,, ,,	New Cross	12.59 ,,	1.1 ,,
49	,, ,,		1.14 ,,	1.18 ,,
51	,, ,,	London Bridge	1.36 ,,	1.33 ,,
52	,, ,,	South Bermondsey	1.43 ,,	1.43 ,,
53	,, ,,	London Bridge	1.50 ,,	1.49 ,,
54	,, ,,	South Bermondsey	1.57 ,,	1.58 ,,
55	,, ,,	London Bridge	2.4 ,,	2.2 ,,
56	,, ,,	New Cross and Honor Oak Park	2.20 ,,	2.15 ,,

DOWN SPECIAL TRAINS TO PENGE L.B. & S.C.R.

No. of train.	Company's train.	From.	Booked arrival time.	Actual time of arrival.
35	L.B. & S.C.R.	Shoreditch	11.13 a.m.	11.13 a.m.
36	,, ,,	,, ,,	11.28 ,,	11.31 ,,
37	G.E.R.	Liverpool Street	11.36 ,,	11.37 ,,
38	L.B. & S.C.R.	Shoreditch	11.43 ,,	11.45 ,,
39	G.E.R.	Liverpool Street	11.51 ,,	11.53 ,,
40	L.B. & S.C.R.	Shoreditch	11.58 ,,	12.0 noon.
41	G.E.R.	Liverpool Street	12.6 p.m.	12.10 p.m.
42	L.B. & S.C.R.	Whitechapel	12.13 ,,	12.15 ,,
43	G.E.R.	Coborn Road	12.21 ,,	12.19 ,,
44	L.B. & S.C.R.	Whitechapel	12.28 ,,	12.29 ,,
45	G.E.R.	Coborn Road	12.36 ,,	12.35 ,,
46	L.B. & S.C.R.	Whitechapel	12.43 ,,	12.41 ,,
48	,, ,,	Shadwell	1.4 ,,	1.2 ,,
50	,, ,,	,, ,,	1.20 ,,	1.13 ,,

The Railway Gazette reported on the time-keeping of the 96 special trains that conveyed about 100,000 children to the Low Level, High Level and adjacent stations on 30th June 1911 for the Coronation Fete. There was some disruption to the normal timetable, as selected running lines were used for berthing purposes during the event. Nearly 90 additional staff were provided. Of the eight other special trains run to convey performers, railway staff and over 300 press representatives, only one was electrically operated. All the childrens trains were steam hauled.

DOWN SPECIAL TRAINS TO THE CRYSTAL PALACE, S.E. & C.R.

Company's train.	From.	Booked arrival time.	Actual time of arrival.
S.E. & C.R.	Greenwich Park	10.50 a.m.	10.48 a.m.
,, ,,	,, ,,	11.5 ,,	10.58 ,,
,, ,,	Woolwich Arsenal	11.16 ,,	11.15 ,,
G.N.R.	Finsbury Park	11.24 ,,	11.25 ,,
S.E. & C.R.	Brixton	11.30 ,,	11.30 ,,
G.N.R.	Finsbury Park	11.36 ,,	11.35 ,,
S.E. & C.R.	St. Paul's	11.42 ,,	11.41 ,,
G.N.R.	Holloway	11.48 ,,	11.50 ,,
S.E. & C.R.	Walworth Road	11.54 ,,	11.55 ,,
,, ,,	Woolwich Arsenal	12 noon.	12 noon.
,, ,,	Battersea Park Road	12.6 p.m.	12.4 p.m.
G.N.R.	Finsbury Park and Holloway	12.12 ,,	12.12 ,,
S.E. & C.R.	Camberwell	12.18 ,,	12.17 ,,
,, ,,	St. Paul's	12.24 ,,	12.21 ,,
G.N.R.	King's Cross	12.30 ,,	12.25 ,,
S.E. & C.R.	Walworth Road	12.36 ,,	12.30 ,,
G.N.R.	King's Cross	12.43 ,,	12.41 ,,
S.E. & C.R.	Victoria	12.48 ,,	12.45 ,,
,, ,,	St. Paul's	12.54 ,,	12.51 ,,
,, ,,	Plumstead	1.0 ,,	12.57 ,,
,, ,,	Brixton	1.6 ,,	1.9 ,,

No. of train.	Company's train.	From.	Booked arrival time.	Actual time of arrival.
25	S.E. & C.R.	Elephant and Castle	1.12 p.m.	1.3 p.m.
26	,, ,,	Battersea Park Road	1.18 ,,	1.17 ,,
27	,, ,,	St. Paul's	1.24 ,,	1.19 ,,
28	G.N.R.	King's Cross	1.30 ,,	1.27 ,,
29	S.E. & C.R.	Camberwell	1.36 ,,	1.33 ,,
30	G.N.R.	King's Cross	1.42 ,,	1.41 ,,
31	S.E. & C.R.	Clapham	1.48 ,,	1.46 ,,
32	,, ,,	Elephant and Castle	1.54 ,,	1.50 ,,
33	,, ,,	Victoria	2.2 ,,	1.59 ,,
34	,, ,,	St. Paul's	2.6 ,,	2.5 ,,
35	,, ,,	Westcombe Park	2.12 ,,	2.9 ,,
36	,, ,,	Nunhead	2.18 ,,	2.13 ,,
37	,, ,,	Catford	2.24 ,,	2.23 ,,
38	,, ,,	Greenwich Park	2.30 ,,	2.28 ,,
39	,, ,,	,, ,,	2.36 ,,	2.35 ,,
40	,, ,,	Catford	2.43 ,,	2.42 ,,

DOWN SPECIAL TRAINS TO SYDENHAM HILL, S.E. & C.R.

No. of train.	Company's train.	From.	Booked arrival time.	Actual time of arrival.
12	Midland	West Hampstead	12.1 p.m.	12.1 p.m.
15	,, ,,	Kentish Town	12.10 ,,	12.14 ,,
23	,, ,,	,, ,,	12.51 ,,	12.52 ,,

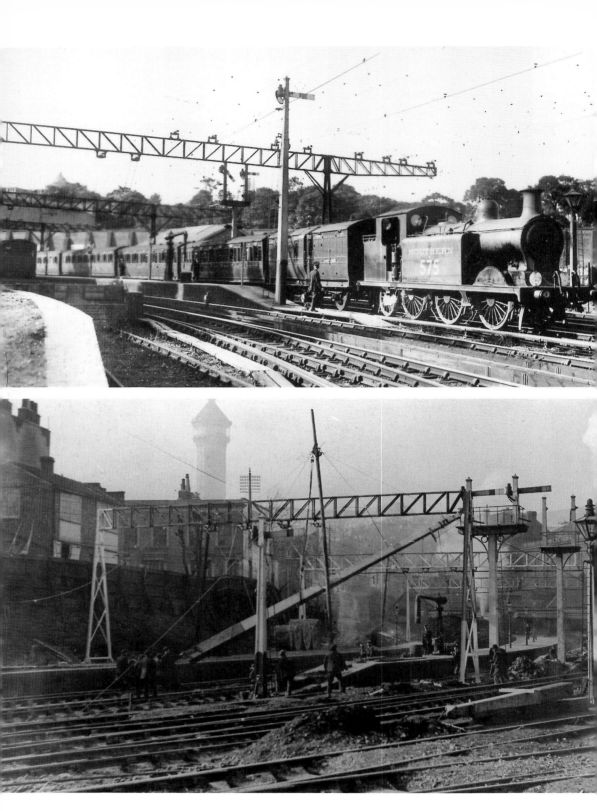

79. The starting signal for platform 6 is off but the train is about three vehicles too long for the driver to see it. The foreman on the walkway is probably about to give verbal instruction to the driver of class E5 no. B575 to proceed. The jib of the 5-ton crane is partly visible.
(Pamlin Prints)

80. This is a flashback to about 1910, as the gantries await wires. The post in the centre of the previous picture is being erected and the bay signals have already been moved forward a few yards, but obviously not far enough for some trains. (G.Gundry coll.)

81. An electric train is at platform 2 while class E5 no. B404 waits at no. 3 on 18th February 1928. The tower in the background was one of two designed by I.K.Brunel to supply the equally spectacular fountains. The former were demolished in 1941 to provide 1600 tons of metal for the war effort. (H.C.Casserley)

82. Smoke lingers at the tunnel mouth in this detailed study of AC overhead equipment suspension design. The starting signal on the right is for restarting trains that have terminated at platform 7. (British Rail)

0028
SOUTHERN RAILWAY.
Available on Day of issue only.
Crystal Palace to
WANDSWORTH COM.
First Class (I.A)
FOR CONDITIONS SEE BACK.
- - - - - - - -
SOUTHERN RAILWAY.
Available on Day of issue only.
Wandsworth Com. to
CRYSTAL PALACE
INCLUDING ADMISSION
First Class
0028

SOUTHERN RLY.
Streatham Hill to
(S.5)
BALHAM and
UPPER TOOTING
Third. Cl. Fare 2½d.
FOR CONDITIONS SEE BACK.
7707

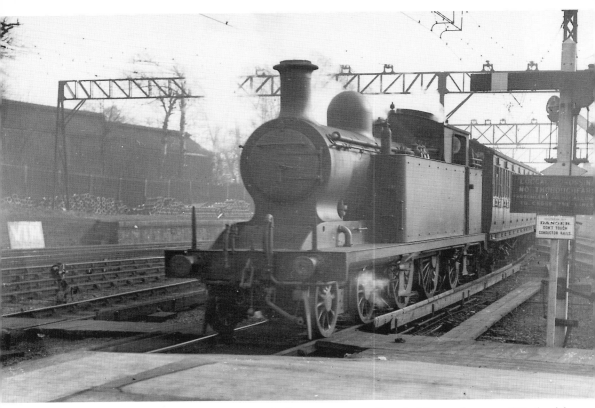

83. Arriving on 18th February 1928 at platform 3 is class I1 4-4-2T no. B10, devoid of a headcode. East Box is largely obscured by the warning board. This class was known as "shy steamers" and this engine was fitted with a larger boiler in the following year. Withdrawal took place in 1948. (H.C.Casserley)

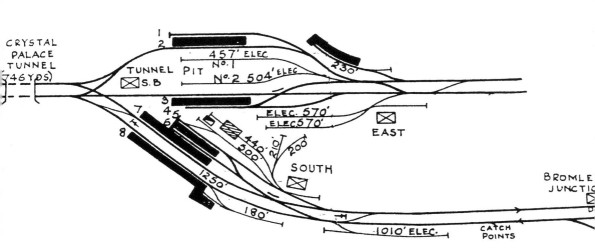

Control diagram from World War II.

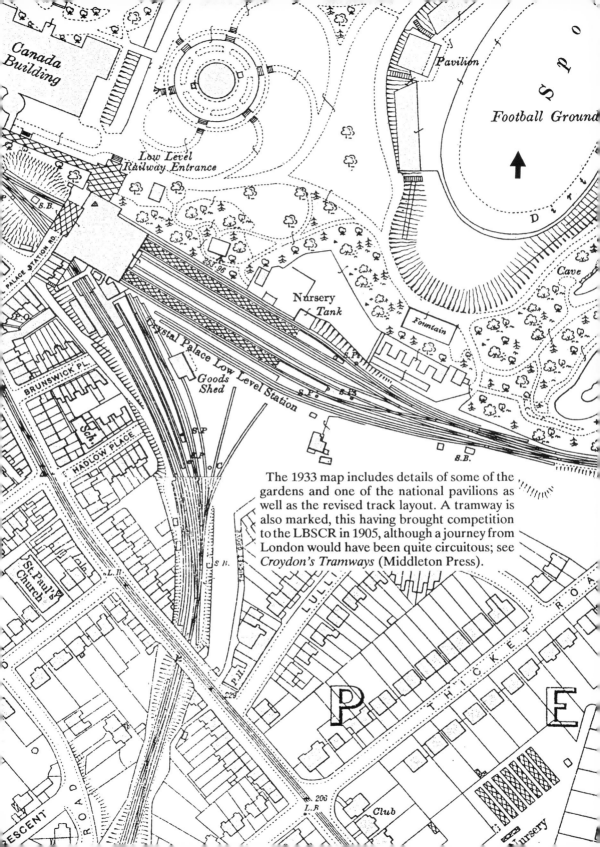

Canada Building

Low Level Railway Entrance

Pavilion

Football Ground

Cave

Nursery Tank

Fountain

Crystal Palace Low Level Station

Goods Shed

BRUNSWICK PL.

HADLOW PLACE

St. Paul's Church

The 1933 map includes details of some of the gardens and one of the national pavilions as well as the revised track layout. A tramway is also marked, this having brought competition to the LBSCR in 1905, although a journey from London would have been quite circuitous; see *Croydon's Tramways* (Middleton Press).

THICKET GROVE

LULLI

THICKET ROA

P

E

Club

Nursery

CRESCENT ROAD

84. The 4.23pm from London Bridge is seen on its circular tour back to that station via Tulse Hill on 20th April 1952. This unusual view of faded elegance includes part of the glazed walkway that once linked the station with the Palace, coupled chimneys, a function-less tapered tower and an ornate porte-cochère with one panel of tracery missing. This shelter stood for at least a further ten years. (J.H.Aston)

85. A look down the steps to platforms 1 and 2 helps to convey the palatial atmosphere of this part of the station. The High Level station closed on 20th September 1954, rendering the words "Low Level" for this station irrelevant. (British Rail)

86. Looking back up the steps one can imagine them thronged with excited visitors emerging from a packed train to witness some unusual entertainment or public spectacle. Speed of train emptying was often critical. (British Rail)

87. A northward view in May 1954 includes the goods shed which was in use until the yard closed on 9th December 1965. The buffer stops are on berthing sidings, not goods lines. (D.Cullum)

88. Passing "B" Box (formerly South Box) on 19th November 1955 is no. 34043 *Combe Martin* with a football excursion from Brockenhurst to Norwood Junction. On the left is the short non-electrified dock siding. November gloom prevails. (S.C.Nash)

89. Passing "C" Box (formerly East Box) on Sunday 30th December 1956 is class E4 no. 32472 with the "Mid Kent Rly and WE&CP Rly Centenarian". Two berthing sidings are in the foreground. (S.C.Nash)

90. "The Kentish Heights Special" emerges from the tunnel behind class O1 no. 31064 on 10th November 1957. It was a ramblers excursion from Greenford to Westerham. "A" Box had been earlier known as "Tunnel" or "Tunnel Mouth". (S.C.Nash)

91. The sidings referred to in captions 87 and 89 are seen in full here in 1969. The wall was on the gigantic scale of the Palace itself. Yellow panels were giving way to yellow ends at this time. (F.Hornby)

92. "C" Box was one of the early eaveless designs of the LBSCR, a notable survivor in 1994 being at Billingshurst. "B" Box was closed on 15th January 1967 when the two bay lines were abolished. "A" and "C" boxes ceased to function on 13th July 1969. (J.Scrace)

Inset: The original roof was recorded in a postcard view, along with the goods shed and two trains of four-wheeled coaches.

London   The Crystal Palace

93. A 1969 view from "C" Box reveals the former roof line. The twin spans were similar to the one at Charing Cross station which suffered catastrophic truss failure in December 1905 (see our *Charing Cross to Dartford* album). The roof here was removed shortly after that event as a precaution. The central supporting wall was also demolished. (J.Scrace)

94. On the right is the stairway that once descended to the very wide central platform. With platforms on both sides of a train, it could be emptied extremely quickly. The loss of the overall roof has for long been mourned. The circular route from London Bridge through platforms 2 and 3 was reduced to peak hours only in May 1974. (Pamlin Prints)

95. To add to the locomotive variety recorded on the route, we include no. 50011 working the 10.55 Acton to Norwood Junction freight on 4th November 1977. The four remaining platforms were then numbered from the south, no. 1 thus being on the left. (J.Scrace)

96. A most unusual locomotive passed through on 21st September 1985, this being ex-London Transport Metropolitan Line *Sarah Siddons* destined for Folkestone West. The rear coupled chimney stacks are evident. (A.Dasi-Sutton)

97. The 13.00 Victoria to Gatwick Airport was diverted via Crystal Palace on 17th February 1988, due to a signal failure at Selhurst, no. 73130 adding further to the traction diversity revealed herein. The rear of the new booking hall can be seen. (J.Scrace)

99. On 7th March 1992, the 13.18 Bedford to Gatwick Airport service was diverted away from London Bridge, owing to engineering work. On the left is a Guildford to Luton train, worked by unit no. 319030. The number of destinations available without change increased greatly with the introduction of such Thameslink trains in May 1988. (C.Wilson)

98. A 1991 picture shows the brave attempt to create a miniature Crystal Palace to accommodate the booking office. The main buildings had become a great liability to BR and were then in commercial use. The "French Chateau" style tower was demolished in October 1976, despite consent being refused owing to its listed status. In court BR successfully pleaded necessity due to storm damage. (V.Mitchell)

100. The inspection saloon no. 975025 is being propelled by no. 73141 through platform 4 on 15th February 1992, as long standing scaffolding protects passengers from the decaying structure above. Great efforts were made in 1971 and again in 1981 to establish a transport museum on this site. The case for moving all exhibits from southern railways to York is still indefensible, particularly as many are not shown. (A.Dasi-Sutton)

101. We make no apology for dwelling upon the unique atmosphere that this historic station can still present. No. 455839 runs from shade to light successively as it rumbles over the junction on 1st July 1993 and proceeds towards West Croydon. (J.Scrace)

102. Seen from the little-used platform 3 on the same day, the hammering of the wheels of no. 456001 echoes through the cavernous space of the palatial structure, so in harmony with the Palace it once served. The photographer is standing close to a discreetly concealed facility for gentlemen. (J.Scrace)

BIRKBECK

103. The station opened on 2nd March 1930, the year after the line was reopened and provided with a frequent service of electric trains. There was no signal box here, the distant arm being that of Norwood Spur Junction box. The spur to Norwood Junction carried passengers until 1st January 1917, freight until 11th September 1959 and closed on 30th October 1966. (H.C.Casserley coll.)

The 1933 edition marks the steps down to Elmers End Road, shown as Clay Lane on earlier editions. By that time housing development was complete within the vicinity of the station.

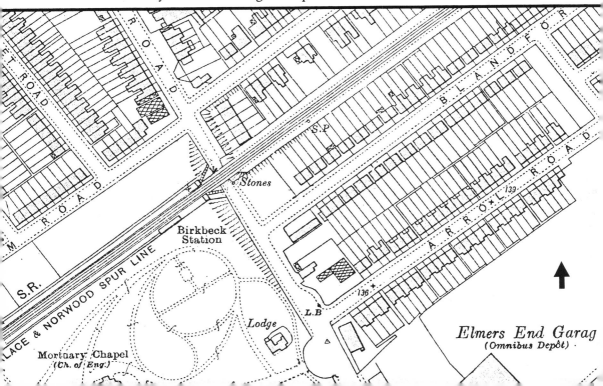

104. Bridge repairs were in progress on 8th December 1962, road traffic being controlled by the amberless temporary lights of that period. The steps to the down platform are on the right. (R.K.Kirkland)

105. A 4SUB unit departs for Beckenham Junction on the same day. Earlier types of train to use the route are shown in picture nos. 76 and 77. SECR steam railcars nos. 5 and 8 also saw intermittent service prior to World War I, but they were unpopular and unreliable. (R.K.Kirkland)

106. The up line was taken out of use between Bromley Junction and Beckenham Junction in February 1983. (Bromley Junction is near Norwood Reservoir on the 1872 6" map). This (and the next picture) was taken on 1st July 1993. (J.Scrace)

107. The 10.37 from Victoria nears the end of its journey despite bearing the words "Smitham via Norbury". The platform on the left may once again be used by passengers when trams commence running to Croydon. (J.Scrace)

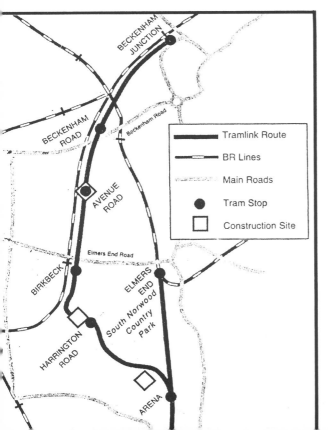

▬▬▬▬	Tramlink Route
▭▭▭▭	BR Lines
⋯⋯⋯	Main Roads
●	Tram Stop
▢	Construction Site

The Act for the Croydon Tramlink received royal assent on 12th July 1994 and commencement of service was planned for 1998. Starting at Wimbledon, the route is described in two of our albums - *Mitcham Junction Lines* (at picture 103) and *London Bridge to Addiscombe* (at picture 120).

BECKENHAM JUNCTION

108. The first station here was used by trains from Lewisham and opened as a terminus on 1st January 1857. It became a through station on 3rd May 1858 when trains started to run between Bromley (now Shortlands) and Crystal Palace. This eastward view is after 1890 when the overall roof was removed. No. 667 has been seen earlier in picture 76. (Lens of Sutton)

109. Another eastward view includes both bay platforms. The one on the right has been used mostly for Crystal Palace line trains, although until 1917 it was also probably used by the Norwood Junction shuttle service. These trains were operated jointly by the LBSCR and LCDR, later the SECR. (Lens of Sutton)

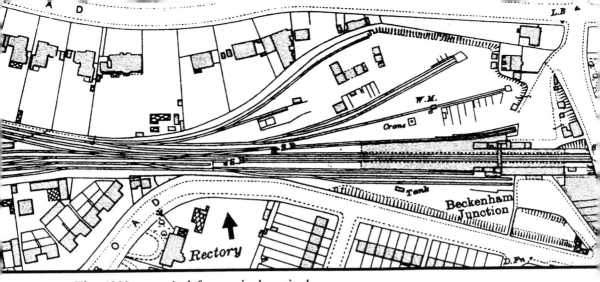

The 1933 survey's left margin has single berthing sidings top and bottom. Between them are the two lines to New Beckenham (top), then the two main lines to Kent House and below them are the two to Crystal Palace. The latter two routes divided further west until 1928 at Penge Junction, having passed over the Lewisham-Elmers End line.

111. A 1957 westward view includes a platform extension at a greater height than the old one and with a safety recess. The staff crossing was subsequently eliminated in the pursuit of safety. (British Rail)

110. An SECR H class 0-4-4T is approaching the station on the main line with an odd assortment of vans behind the coaches. The single electrified line in the foreground leads to the up bay. (S.A.W.Harvey/R.C.Riley coll.)

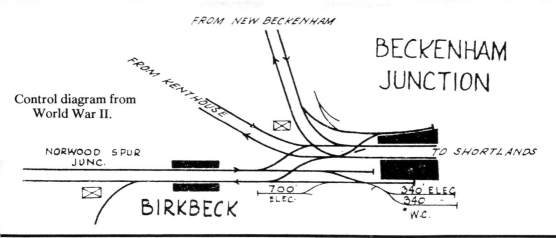

BECKENHAM
JUNCTION

FROM NEW BECKENHAM

FROM KENTHOUSE

NORWOOD SPUR
JUNC.

BIRKBECK

TO SHORTLANDS

700'
ELEC.

340' ELEC
340 "
W.C.

112. The 10.45am Herne Hill to Ramsgate calls to pick up holidaymakers on 30th August 1958. The locomotive is N class 2-6-0 no. 31810. This train, which only ran on summer Saturdays, called here at 10.58am and arrived at Ramsgate at 1.32pm. (N.L.Browne)

113. A closer look at the up starting signals on the same day reveals that preparations are well advanced for their demise. On the right is a new bracket and in the distance is a new signal box. (N.L.Browne)

114. The last Beckenham Junction box was in use controlling colour light signals from 12th April 1959 until 13th April 1983. This photograph of it was taken in 1982. (J.Scrace)

115. The down side buildings were recorded in the 1960s, the structure probably having reached its centenary by then. Prior to 1899 the station was worked jointly by the LCDR and the SER, a rare example of co-operation between the rivals. (British Rail)

116. The down side buildings were modest in comparison with those on the up side. On the right is the sign *GOODS DEPOT*. This was in use for general traffic until 18th April 1964. Ricketts used the yard as a coal concentration depot from 1966 until 1982, using a distinctive yellow-painted 0-4-0 Fowler diesel for shunting. (British Rail)

117. Platform 1, the bay for Crystal Palace line trains, was photographed in 1987. Structural damage was caused here on 1st November 1985 when a terminating class 455 unit developed brake failure. (P.Davis)

118. The smartly maintained south elevation was pictured in July 1990. The land on the left had earlier been used for two berthing sidings but prior to 1929 was used for a second goods yard, probably once that of the LCDR. (J.Scrace)

119. Approaching platform 3 at speed on 10th August 1990 is no. 47851 with the 07.59 Liverpool Lime Street to Folkestone Central service. Platform 4 (right) was used for terminating stopping trains from Victoria via Kent House. The spur to New Beckenham was singled by then and no longer carried a regular passenger service. (J.Scrace)

LONDON BRIDGE, CRYSTAL PALACE, and VICTORIA.—London, Brighton, and South Coast.

Week Days.

(timetable)

Week Days—Continued. / Sundays.

(timetable)

Stations: City Station, London Bridge dep, New Cross, Brockley *, Honor Oak Park, Forest Hill †, Sydenham, Crystal Palace ‡, Gipsy Hill ‡, West Norwood, Streatham Hill, Balham § [mon, Wandsworth Com., Clapham Jun. 153, Battersea Park, Grosvenor Road, Victoria (W. E.) arr

a To London Bridge, via West Norwood and Tulse Hill Spur Line,　　**b** Workmen's Cheap Trains.
* Station for Upper New Cross and Nunhead; † for Lordship Lane; ‡ for Upper Norwood; § Balham and Upper Tooting.

VICTORIA, CRYSTAL PALACE, and LONDON BRIDGE.—London, Brighton, and South Coast.

Week Days.

(timetable)

Week Days—Continued. / Sundays.

(timetable)

Stations: West End Sta., Victoria dep, Grosvenor Road, Battersea Park, Clapham Junc. 159, Wandsworth Com., Balham § [mon, Streatham Hill, West Norwood, Gipsy Hill ‡, Crystal Palace ‡, Sydenham, Forest Hill †, Honor Oak Park, Brockley *, New Cross, London Bridge arr

December 1902

→ 120. This connection from the up main line to the Birkbeck route, seen in 1994, gave another diversionary link, in addition to the spur mentioned in the previous caption. At that time, both routes had a basic service of two trains per hour but many more at peak times. (V. Mitchell)

Other views of this busy and historic station, together with earlier maps, can be seen in our *Victoria to Bromley South* album.

● *Other Local Railway albums* ●

London Bridge to East Croydon

Victoria to Bromley South

Waterloo to Windsor

Waterloo to Woking

Crystal Palace (High Level) and Catford Loop

Holborn Viaduct to Lewisham

London Bridge to Addiscombe
including Hayes Branch

Mitcham Junction Lines
from Peckham Rye, West Croydon, Sutton and Wimbledon

West Croydon to Epsom
including Epsom Downs Branch

Clapham Junction to Beckenham Junction
including Crystal Palace (Low Level)

● *Local Tramway albums* ●

Camberwell and West Norwood Tramways

Lewisham and Catford Tramways

Southwark and Deptford Tramways

Write for our full list of Railway, Tramway and Waterway,
Military, Bus and Local History albums and books

Easebourne Lane, Midhurst, West Sussex. GU29 9AZ
Tel: (0730) 813169 Fax: (0730) 812601